Ex Libris

Library of Congress Cataloging-in-Publication Data

Thayer, Ernest Lawrence, 1863-1940.
  [Casey at the bat]
  Ernest L. Thayer's Casey at the bat: a ballad of the Republic
  sung in the year 1888 / seriously and faithfully illustrated
  by Christopher Bing. 1st ed.
    p. cm.
  ISBN: 1-929766-00-9
  1. Casey, Brian Kavanagh, 1859-1946 Poetry. 2. Baseball
  players Poetry. 3. Baseball Poetry. I. Title: Casey
  at the bat. II. Bing, Christopher H. III. Title.
  PS3014.T3 C3 2000
  811'.52 dc21

  00-037010

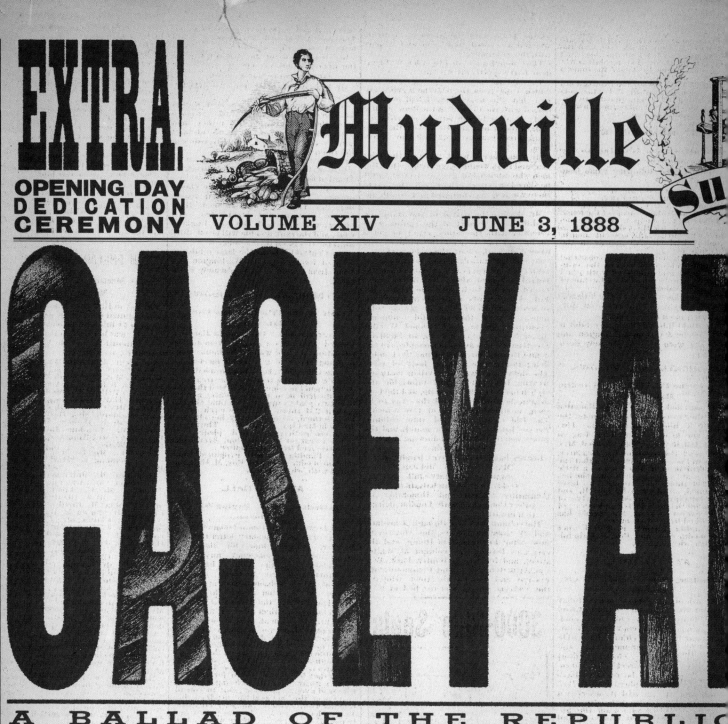

EXTRA!

OPENING DAY DEDICATION CEREMONY

Mudville SU[...]

VOLUME XIV   **JUNE 3, 1888**

CASEY AT [

A BALLAD OF THE REPUBLIC

REPORTED BY ERNEST L. THAYE[

Illustrations ©2000 by Christopher Bing
All rights reserved

Published by Handprint Books 413 Sixth Avenue Brooklyn, New York 11215

Printed in China

FIRST EDITION

ISBN 1-929766-00-9

10 9 8 7 6 5 4 3 2 1

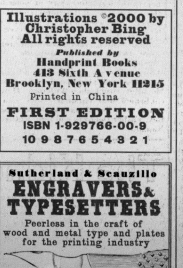
A NOTE TO THE READER...

...about the second signature on the illustrations which appears in the lower right hand corner of each spread.

Until late in the 19th century, the metal plates from which newspaper illustrations were printed were prepared by hand by craftsmen known as engravers. Their skill lay in translating the light and shadows of the artist's original drawing on paper into the precise, unforgiving line cut into zinc or copper plates. Some of these engravers were merely crude copyists, others displayed keen talent and an interpretive gift which often augmented the artist's intention (and even covered his flaws). Over time, several of the engravers became famous in the[ir] own right, and their work was sought after as that of the arti[st] whose images they reproduced. [It] was custom for the original artist['s] name to appear in the lower le[ft] of the engraving; the engraver['s] name, when allowed, appeared [in] the lower right.

(Continued on front end papers)

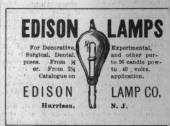

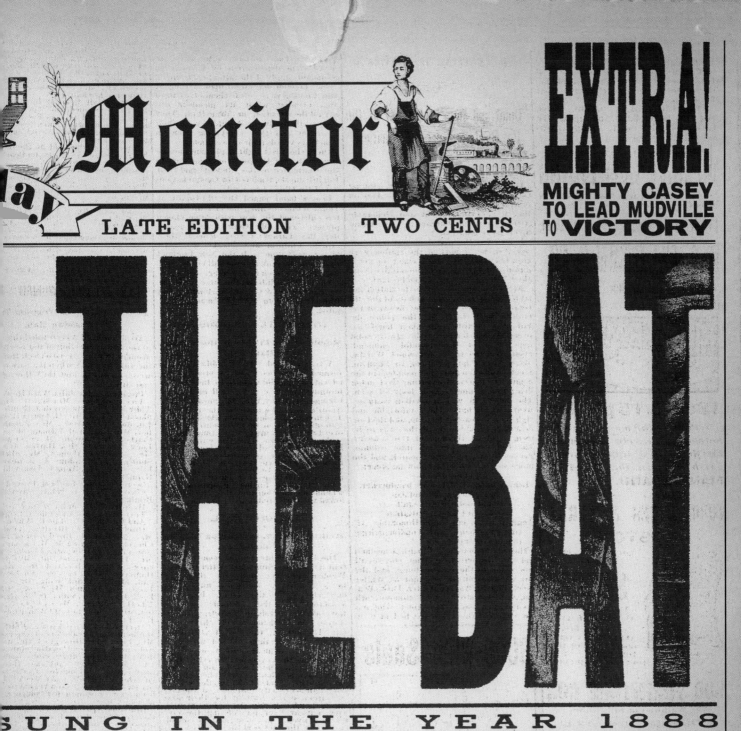

Monitor

LATE EDITION   TWO CENTS

EXTRA!

MIGHTY CASEY TO LEAD MUDVILLE TO **VICTORY**

THE BAT

SUNG IN THE YEAR 1888

ILLUSTRATED BY CHRISTOPHER BING

THANKS & ACKNOWLEDGEMENTS

Martin Gardner's brilliant and entertaining *The Annotated Casey at the Bat* is the source for the title and stanzas in this version of Casey, which is exactly how it was first published Sunday morning, June 3rd, 1888 in the *San Francisco Examiner*.

Wallace Tripp's wonderfully illustrated version (Coward, McCann and Geoghegan, Inc., New York) in 1978 was/is the inspiration for this version and should be print again.

This book (and those to follow) could not have happened without the moral support and a helpful word on my behalf by Dr. Henry Louis Gates Jr.

Carl Brandt, my agent, for listening to the helpful word and stepping out of his usual arena and into another on my behalf, and being more interested in my getting it right than the many deadlines that came and went (due to family needs), and the bottom line (and his son, who has fought for me in another artistic arena for years helping to support my venture into this one, none of us knowing, until recently, of our professional relationships with each other).

Christopher Franceschelli, my publisher, who backed this rookie and believed in this book since he first saw sketches eight years ago.

My wife, Wendy, and our children, who have to beware of the bear in the barn, but they keep feeding it anyway, and spend so much time going without.

My parents who keep a hope and faith (in me) alive that would put Boston Red Sox or Chicago Cubs fans to shame.

My in-laws who actually admit that I'm family, and Gil Barrett (my brother-in-law) who put up with my turning him from the best mechanic in New England into THE model for Casey. Finding the world of modeling too dull, he has happily returned to being the best mechanic in New England.

Joseph and Princes Fludd who gave me friendship, food, and shelter one very cold and snowy night on my way to do research at the Baseball Hall of Fame.

The Baseball Hall of Fame in Cooperstown, New York and all the people who work in their photo

(Continued on front end papers)

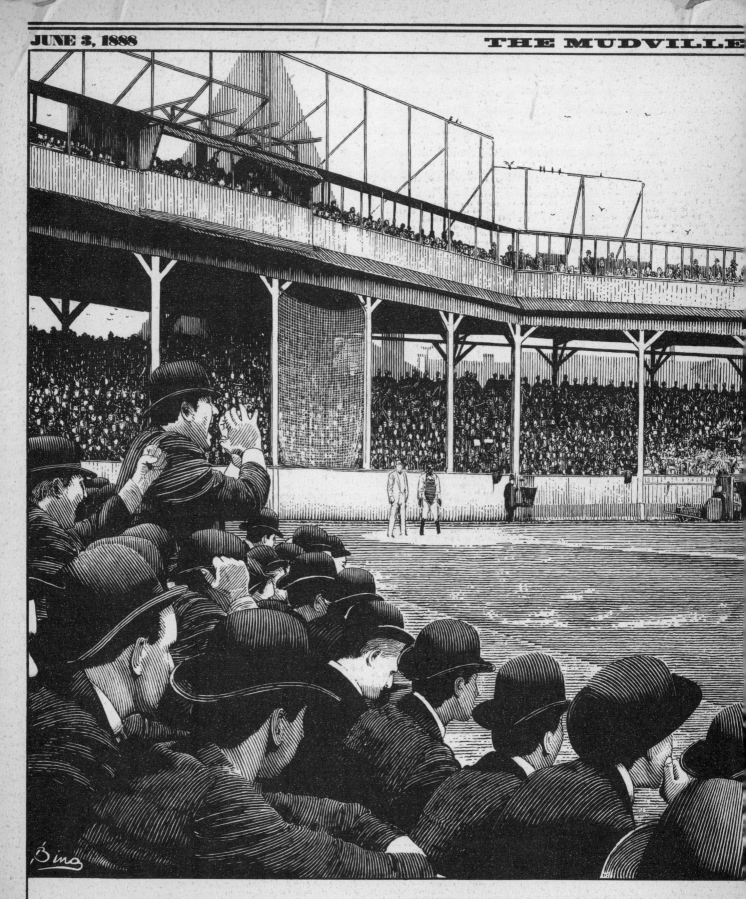

The outlook wasn't brilliant for the Mudville nine that day;
The score stood four to two with but one inning more to play.

And then when Cooney died at first, and Barrows did the same,
A sickly silence fell upon the patrons of the game.

ss themselves as delighted with their
tion and that everything seen in
rica exceeds their expectations.

the boat last night a pleasant episode
an elegant banquet complimentary to
committee of the Ancients and their
ish guests, tendered by George L. Con-

after which all present knelt while a wedding hymn was sung. Mendelssohn's
wedding march was played as the couple
left the church.

A reception was held at the residence of
Mrs. Nathaniel W. Curtis, on Beacon street,
after the ceremony.

Among those who were present were:
Mrs. N. W. Curtis,   Mr. A   on,

CUSTOMS DECISIONS.

Two Circulars from Washington Re-
ceived by the Collector.

This forenoon the following came from
Washington:

has concurred with the Board of Aldermen
upon the appropriation bill rather than
stop public business caused by the obstruc-
tionists of the board—eight Republican
aldermen—it is

Resolved, That the appropriation bill, as
it was originally sent to the Board of Aldermen was perfectly legal and right, and its

A straggling few got up to go in deep despair. The rest
Clung to that hope which springs eternal in the human breast;

pile-house and for myself I accept it with loyalty and in that faith."

Debut of American Singers.
(Copaso.)

LONDON, June 2 — Howard Paul introduced two young American vocalists at the concert in St. James' Hall last evening.

man Scott as an enemy of labor, as a dangerous person to the welfare of society and the lately trial progress of America, and as a bitter enemy of organized labor.

SIXTY-SIX LASTERS QUIT.

Stowe, Bills & Hawley's Union Men Refuse to Work with Non-Unionists.

Arthur had paid remarkable deference, breaking the Indiana slate in order to fetch him to Washington, nevertheless served in two departments, and yet was able to make his address for Blaine, while Arthur was sulking under his defeat.

The silly plea that a convention of common sense men must decide against anybody whom the mugwumps do not insult and

man. It would be a confess on that this ticket had be a unsuccessful. That not the case; and while I know that who will vote for him don't like Blaine, there is nothing else to be done.

William Armstrong, postmaster of Oakland, an old democrat, remarked: Judge Thurman: "The Ohio delegation a few votes, I think, for Black; some for Stevenson, and a small number

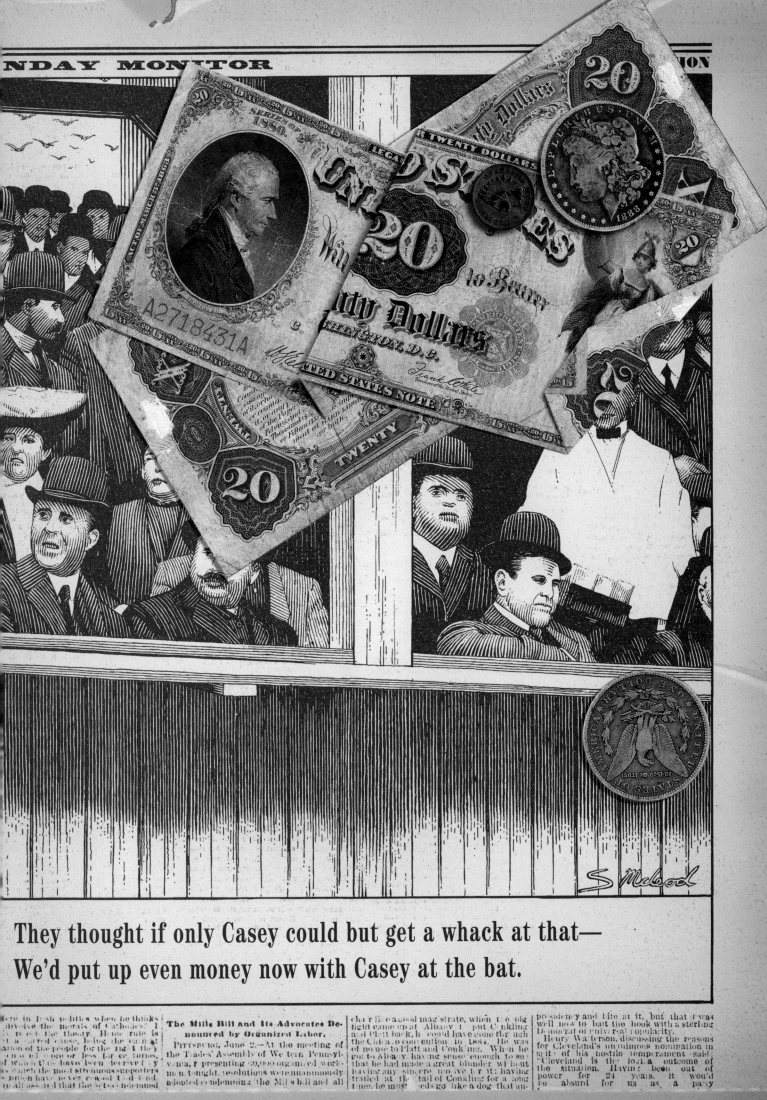

They thought if only Casey could but get a whack at that—
We'd put up even money now with Casey at the bat.

But Flynn preceded Casey, as did also Jimmy Blake,
And the former was a lulu and the latter was a cake;

SURGING FANS SPARK NEAR RIOT

SCORE CAST IN DOUBT WHEN BALL ROLLS INTO CROWD

MANAGERS AND CITY OFFICIALS RENEW CRY FOR BUILDING OF OUTFIELD FENCES

Richloam--Saturday, June 2
Martin Stone's slam into left looked to be a solid double for the Mudville nine in yesterday afternoon's game against the Richloam Roosters. Then the ball hit an obstruction in the grass and began rolling towards the crowd watching from the sidelines. Some twenty Mudville fans crossed onto the field, placed the ball into protective custody and physically prevented Regis Smallwood, the Rooster's leftfielder, from apprehending the ball.

Richloam fans were understandably incensed and exercised swift revenge, attacking the visiting Mudville fans with a flurry of walking sticks. At least one Mudville fan was seen hobbling off the field with a bloodied shirt and blackened eye. Only the quick attention of the local constab-

MAYOR STONE VOICES OUTRAGE

The incident prompted Mayor Sam Stone to make a renewed call for the erection of a wall separating fans from the field. While such a barrier would be a novelty to the game--rumor has it that something of the sort has been built in New York--it is hoped that this action might lead to greater crowd safety and less confusion on the field. More than one fan, however, was heard to say that an artificial barricade would severely curtail the enjoyment of the game and might mean dance. O

So upon that stricken multitude grim melancholy sat,
For there seemed but little chance of Casey's getting to the bat.

would only say:
came here to listen to Indiana in the matter of the vice-presidency. If, however, our it is ready toward Thurman, I should be inclined to go with it."

Mr. Scott avers that he knows nothing of anything in his inside pocket.

The arrival of William H. Barnum of

Bennett Pike, M. J. Kenedick, Rhode Island; Edward D. Landers, chairman; John D. Finley, Charles Rice, Richard Ennis, M. Heller, Thomas M. Taylor, Marcus A. Wolf, Vermont. Judge E. B. Adams, chairman; F. A. Churchill, G. H. Dennison, Henry G. Pasehell, James L. Blair, Marshall Carr, John F. Lee, Jr., W. C. McCreary, George M. Fascheil.

first district Democrats that I am aware of. So far as the presidential election is concerned, I shall vote for Grover Cleveland if nominated, and I believe he will be, I think Thurman will occupy the second place on the ticket."

A Presbyterian paper published in Portland, in a recent editorial, insinuated that Mr. Emery is extremely parsimonious

Michael Gannon. The fire was caused by the upsetting of a kerosene lamp.

--The alarm from box 7 at 8:27 o'clock last night was for a fire at 3 Poplar street, caused by rats and matches. The building which is owned by Peabody & Briggs and occupied by William Laverty, was damaged to the extent of $200.

--Patrolman William J. Innis of station

But Flynn let drive a single, to the wonderment of all,
And Blake, the much despis-ed, tore the cover off the ball;

Another Frenchman who has taken a
very prominent part in recent politics,
Frederick Coudert, is a noted lawyer in
New York, who has a brother of
almost equal ability, and the two
were the sons of a French
school teacher in New York who kept an
academy, and who entertained Louis Napoleon during his brief visit to this country
about 36 years ago. Mr. Cauda says that
his father took Louis Napoleon out on a sea

Some people see Postmaster General
Dickinson as a dark horse selected behind
the Thurman boom. It will be extremely
interesting to watch the movement if it
should be turned away from the loved Ohio.
A big man told him today that there is not
a county in the United States where Thurman's name on the ticket would not add a
few votes. Another man was sure that
the old man's disposition toward the Green-
backers would make a

**Maryland's Delegation will Support
Him for the Vice Presidency.**

St. Louis, June 2.—The Maryland delegation held a meeting at the Southern Hotel
this afternoon, and talked over the question as to the candidate which it would support for the second place on the national
Democratic ticket. The general sentiment

wick They came to Boston to at-
Appleton Mather wedding yesterday
Church of St. John the Evangelist.
James Phillips Jr., a large woolen
facturer of Fitchburg, makes his
Young's when in Boston. He re-
there last evening.

Local Lines.
—Park's British Bitter Beer at H

OF THE BALL

And when the dust had lifted, and the men saw what had occurred,
There was ~~Johnnie~~ safe at second and Flynn a-hugging third.

Jimmy

same combination, and Cl veland is
sure Tilden's heir. Frank Blair g
the United States Senate for one te
he died, wi h his mind all shattered, in
possession of a city office.
understand that Mrs. Blair is still living
with a grown up family of ver we
been poor until the gove.nment re-
ly gave her a pension, aft r long wait-

chemo of Tax Reduction
now pending in Congress should be mentioned in the platform. By such people it
is thought to be sufficient squarely to in-
dorse the message f the President and
earnestly urge upon C gress the execution
of the princ ple. The New York platform
is really liked by Mr. Cleveland better than that of

PROOFREADER SOUGHT
THE MUDVILLE MONITOR seeks proofreader for immediate hire due to last
incumbent's sudden departure. The successful
candidate shall possess an exquisite command
of the language, display meticulous attention
to detail while working to extreme deadlines,
be impervious to the bustle of a cacophonous

in their power.

Kansas Men Favor Cresham.
TOPEKA, Kan., June 2.—A canvass of the
18 delegates from Kansas to the Chicago
convention since Mr. Blaine's last
letter shows that Gresham is the
personal preference of the ma-
One delegate is for Davis.

Then from 5,000 throats and more there rose a lusty yell;
It rumbled through the valley, it rattled in the dell;

It knocked upon the mountain and recoiled upon the flat,
For Casey, mighty Casey, was advancing to the bat.

There was ease in Casey's manner as he stepped into his place;
There was pride in Casey's bearing and a smile on Casey's face.

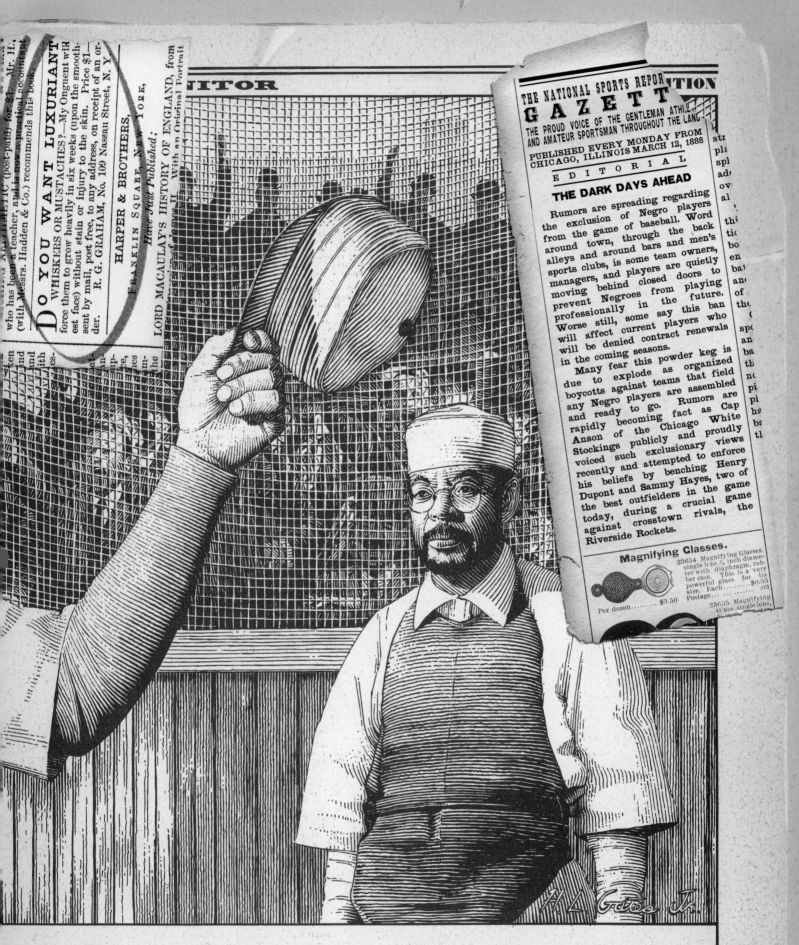

And when, responding to the cheers, he lightly doffed his hat,
No stranger in the crowd could doubt 'twas Casey at the bat.

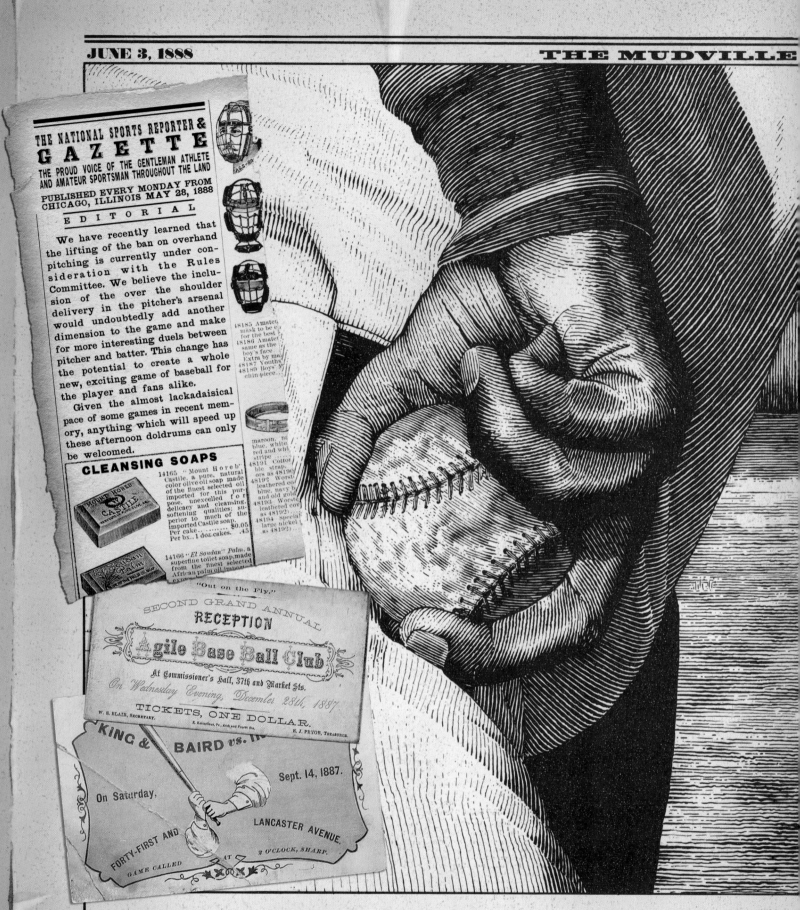

THE NATIONAL SPORTS REPORTER &
GAZETTE
THE PROUD VOICE OF THE GENTLEMAN ATHLETE AND AMATEUR SPORTSMAN THROUGHOUT THE LAND

PUBLISHED EVERY MONDAY FROM CHICAGO, ILLINOIS MAY 28, 1888

EDITORIAL

We have recently learned that the lifting of the ban on overhand pitching is currently under consideration with the Rules Committee. We believe the inclusion of the over the shoulder delivery in the pitcher's arsenal would undoubtedly add another dimension to the game and make for more interesting duels between pitcher and batter. This change has the potential to create a whole new, exciting game of baseball for the player and fans alike.

Given the almost lackadaisical pace of some games in recent memory, anything which will speed up these afternoon doldrums can only be welcomed.

CLEANSING SOAPS

14165 "Mount Horeb" Castile, a pure, natural color olive oil soap made of the finest selected oil imported for this purpose, unexcelled for delicacy and cleansing, softening qualities, superior to much of the imported Castile soap.
Per cake............ $0.05
Per bx.. 1 doz. cakes. .45

14166 "El Soudan" Palm, a superfine toilet soap, made from the finest selected African palm oil imported.

"Out on the Fly."

SECOND GRAND ANNUAL
RECEPTION
Agile Base Ball Club
At Commissioner's Hall, 37th and Market Sts.
On Wednesday Evening, December 28th, 1887.
TICKETS, ONE DOLLAR.
W. S. BLAIR, SECRETARY.
E. J. PRYOR, TREASURER.

KING & BAIRD vs.
On Saturday,
Sept. 14, 1887.
FORTY-FIRST AND
LANCASTER AVENUE.
GAME CALLED AT 2 O'CLOCK, SHARP.

Ten thousand eyes were on him as he rubbed his hands with dirt;
Five thousand tongues applauded when he wiped them on his shirt.

THE NATIONAL SPORTS REPORTER &
GAZETTE EDITION
THE PROUD VOICE OF THE GENTLEMAN ATHLETE
AND AMATEUR SPORTSMAN THROUGHOUT THE LAND
PUBLISHED EVERY MONDAY FROM
CHICAGO, ILLINOIS APRIL 9, 188

EDITORIAL

PANSIES IN THE (OUT)FIELD

The hoots and cat calls "Mama's boy," "Cake" and "Lulu" often heard from the sidelines of late are the fans' justified response to the recent introduction of the ball glove to the great American pastime. They justifiably see this move as a disgrace-perhaps the first step in the calculated and tragic emasculation of the game. Blisters and swollen hands, once

Base Ball Gloves.

48149 Special Baseman's Glove, heavy oil tanned goat skin, extra heavy, padded; full left hand not tipped, right hand fingerless, hand sewed, warranted.
Per pair...... $1.50
Extra by mail, 10 cents
48150 Boys' Gloves, fingerless, open backs padded......... .20

Short Fingers,
Extra by mail

48149

regarded as well-earned battle scars and tell-tale signs of a player's brawn and guts, are cited by supporters as reasons for the ball glove's necessity. Jake Goodwin, shortstop for Lesterville, shamelessly admits he is in favor of the new accessory: "Day in, day out, your hands get really torn up and it is hard to grip the bat tightly with all the bandages." Most fans and players argue that swollen hands and jammed fingers are part of the sport, badges of honor worn proudly by our summer warriors. "It's a man's game after all," says one fan, "and anyone who disagrees can start a splinter collection on the bench." This sentiment is not limited to the stands. Ronald Ferguson, veteran catcher for Dunston, is equally adamant: "It gets a lot easier after three innings or so because the swelling numbs your hands and tends to act like cushioning. It ain't nothing to get bothered over, nothing a real man can't handle." Amazingly, the ball glove, despite overwhelming, level-headed opposition, seems to be gaining gradual acceptance. What's next? Outfielders with parasols? Helmets for base runners? Women players?

Then while the writhing pitcher ground the ball into his hip,
Defiance gleamed in Casey's eye, a sneer curled Casey's lip.

And now the leather-covered sphere came hurtling through the air,
And Casey stood a-watching it in haughty grandeur there.

PUBLISHED EVERY MON
CHICAGO, ILLINOIS

LETTERS TO THE EDI

Sir:

I would like to r
disagree with your
absolutely absurd sugg
lifting the overhand
would be good for the
delivery has been ba
baseball for some time
good reason! Any thinkin
should realize that the offense will
suffer greatly should the ban be
lifted and the game will be
stripped of any semblance of fair
play. With such an unlimited
sphere of delivery, along with the
added power put upon the ball, the
overhand pitch gives the defense
all the power.

Mudville Center Celebration, June 3, 1888
ARTISTICVIEW
Balloon inflation ceremony

only possible remedy for
this outrageous travesty of justice
would be to move the pitcher's
box back ten feet from its present
position. This would allow the
batter to have more time to react
and up the probability of actually
making contact with the ball.

Certainly, no serious fan of the
sport would deny that home runs
and line drives are what make
baseball exciting--no one goes to
the park to see strike outs and
no-hitters. Unless the overhand
pitch is coupled with the shifted
pitcher's box, reinstating the
overhand pitch will completely
ruin baseball. If it isn't broken,
gentlemen...Don't Try To Fix It!

C. Franceschelli

Close by the sturdy batsman the ball unheeded sped—
"That ain't my style," said Casey. "Strike one," the umpire said.

Rescript Finds a Defender in a
Liberal M. P.

Walking Down the Road, Cowie and
McQuaid Overtook Her.

Bing

From the benches, black with people, there went up a muffled roar,
Like the beating of the storm-waves on a stern and distant shore.

REVOLVERS.

In accordance with the following extract we cannot sell a *minor* resident of the State of Illinois a revolver. This law does not apply to any State except Illinois.

Extract from Illinois State Laws.

PAR. 2b. Whoever, not being the father, guardian or employer of the minor herein named, by himself or agent, shall sell, give, loan, hire or barter to any minor within this State, any pistol, revolver, derringer, bowie knife or dirk or other deadly weapon of like character capable of being secreted upon the person, shall be guilty of misdemeanor and shall be fined in any sum not less than twenty-five dollars nor more than two hundred dollars.

NOTICE.

TO RESIDENTS OF ILLINOIS ONLY.

If you live in any other State, you do not have to send the "Sample Letter."

Orders for revolvers to residents of the State of Illinois must be accompanied with a letter embracing all the points contained in the following "SAMPLE LETTER." The purchaser will of course substitute his own name, residence, age and purpose for which the arm is required, and also obtain two witnesses. Attention is called to the extract from the Illinois State laws above. A minor cannot buy a revolver, but his father, guardian or employer can buy it for him. This law applies to the residents of Illinois only.

"SAMPLE LETTER."

MESSRS. MONTGOMERY WARD & CO., CHICAGO, ILL. Sept. 1, 1890.
Gentlemen: I wish to purchase a revolver of you. To enable you to comply with the laws of the State of Illinois, I make the following statement:

JOHN DOE. I reside at Windsor Park, Ill. My name is ———. I want the revolver for self-protection.
JOHN DOE.

This is to certify that we, the undersigned, legal voters of the State of Illinois, are personally acquainted with the aforesaid John Doe and believe the above statement made by him to be correct in every particular.
JOHN BROWN, Witness.
ALBERT JONES, Witness.

REVOLVERS.—The following quotations do not include cartridges.

Revolvers can be sent by mail ...

Revolvers—Continued.

47037 Blue Jack-et, No. 1½, a fine shooter, .22 caliber, long or short cartridges, round barrel, rubberstock, full nickel plate, saw handle, length of barrel, 2½ inches; entire length, 6 inches; weight, well rifled, and a good one. Price, each, 7 shot, $1.35. By mail, ...

47039 ... ber, long or sho ... inch barrel, weigh ... nickel plate, entire length, 6 ... rifled barrels. Price ... Using No. 47109-70-71 cartrid ... Extra by mail, 15c. Safe and ...

Rifled Barrel.

47044 Revolver, .22 caliber, rim fire, short or long cartridge, full nickel plate, 2½ inch octagon barrel, flu ... cylinder, rubber saw handles, entire len ... 5½ inches; weight 7 ounces, well made ... durable, 6 shot ... $1 ...

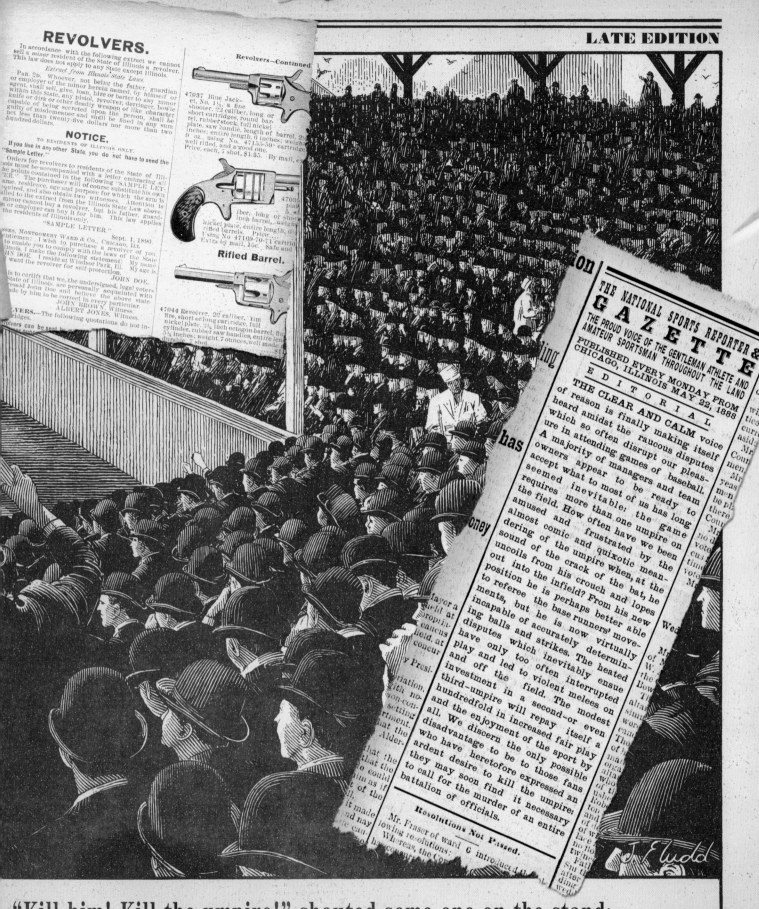

THE NATIONAL SPORTS REPORTER & GAZETTE

THE PROUD VOICE OF THE GENTLEMAN ATHLETE AND AMATEUR SPORTSMAN THROUGHOUT THE LAND

PUBLISHED EVERY MONDAY FROM CHICAGO, ILLINOIS MAY 22, 1888

EDITORIAL

THE CLEAR AND CALM voice of reason is finally making itself heard amidst the raucous disputes which so often disrupt our pleasure in attending games of baseball. A majority of managers and team owners appear to be ready to accept what to most of us has long seemed inevitable: the game requires more than one umpire on the field. How often have we been amused and frustrated by the almost comic and quixotic meandering of the umpire when, at the sound of the crack of the bat, he uncoils from his crouch and lopes out into the infield? From his new position he is perhaps better able to referee the base runners' movements, but he is now virtually incapable of accurately determining balls and strikes. The heated disputes which inevitably ensue have only too often interrupted play and led to violent melees on and off the field. The modest investment in a second-or even third-umpire will repay itself a hundredfold in increased fair play and the enjoyment of the sport by all. We discern the only possible disadvantage to be to those fans who have heretofore expressed an ardent desire to kill the umpire: they may soon find it necessary to call for the murder of an entire battalion of officials.

Resolutions Not Passed.

Mr. Fraser of ward 6 introduced ... lowing resolutions: Whereas, the Co ...

"Kill him! Kill the umpire!" shouted some one on the stand;
And it's likely they'd have killed him had not Casey raised his hand.

With a smile of Christian charity great Casey's visage shone;
He stilled the rising tumult; he bade the game go on;

OLD JUDGE Cigarettes

—Gunning.   COPYRIGHTED, 1887.
Catcher,
Philadelphia.
GOODWIN & CO., NEW YORK.

D. B. CASTLE,
Watchmaker and
JEWELER,
Wholesale and Retail Dealer in
Gold & Silver Watches,
Silver Ware, Fancy Goods, &c.
199 Main Street, Mudville.
Two doors above Exchange St.

Casey paid for old Silver, and great
bargains given in Second Hand
Watches. Watch Repair-
ing done in the best
manner and warranted.

CHAMPIONS OF 1887.

MUDVILLE BASE BALL CLUB

1. CASEY—Rightfield
2. JONES—Pitcher
3. O'TOOLE—Catcher
4. BARROWS—First Base
5. PERONE—Second Base
6. BLAKE—Third Base
7. COONEY—Shortstop
8. FLYNN—Leftfield
9. RABENSKY—Centerfield

JOHN WENDELL,
—DEALER IN—
Mens' Furnishing Goods,
{SHIRTS}
To Order a Specialty,
351 MAIN STREET,
Between N. Division and Eagle,
Mudville, USA

He signaled to the pitcher, and once more the spheroid flew; But Casey still ignored it, and the umpire said, "Strike two."

The Mugwumps' Candidate
is rapidly dissolving. It is true that the Republicans need, and are highly needed
enough to present a contrast to former
campaigns, in which they were worsted;
but no one can find in Gresham's record
a single wavering line toward party
allegiance. Had he been an in-

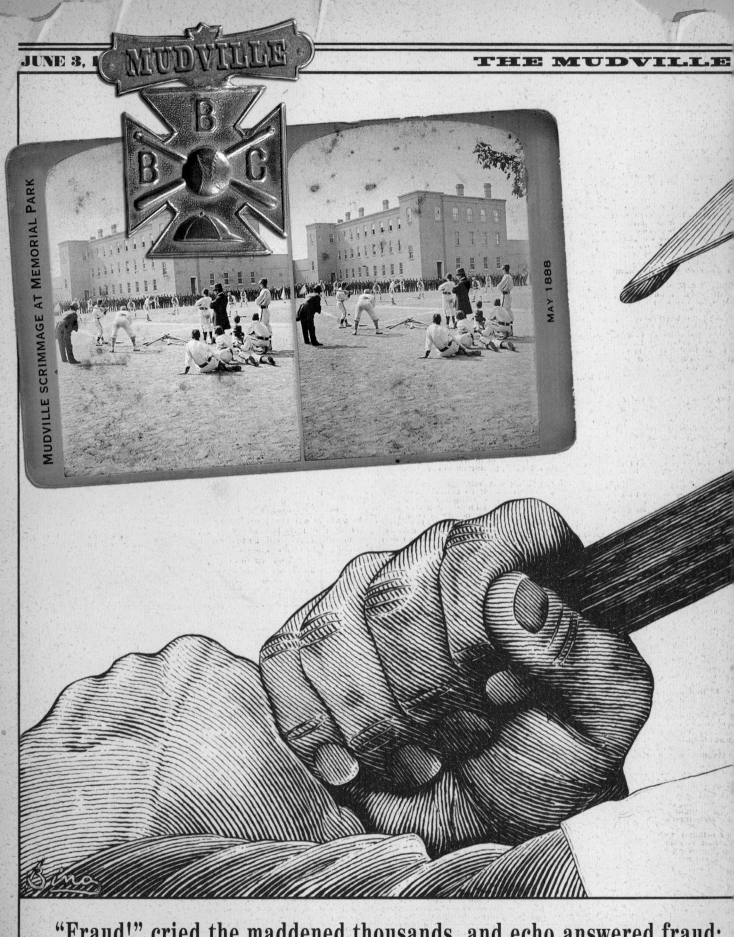

MUDVILLE SCRIMMAGE AT MEMORIAL PARK

MAY 1888

"Fraud!" cried the maddened thousands, and echo answered fraud;
But one scornful look from Casey and the audience was awed.

Wedding at the Church of St. John the Evangelist.

Mrs. Helen Mixter of Beacon street, niece of Mrs. Nathaniel W. Curtis, and Randolph W. Appleton of New York were married at the Church of St. John the Evangelist, on

the ship.

IN HONOR OF R. D. SMITH.

Meeting of the Boston Bar to Take Action on His Death.

There was a meeting of the bar this morn-

brooks they may hold communion with daisies. Perhaps with Claribel and Lillian they will not have time to tell the wrong they have done their fellow by their actions. But time levels all the and the men unjustly treated may hone. All else I envy is that in their

Mudville 11; Salem, 7.

Mudville May 31.—Salem lost today's game on account of an unlucky error by Long in the first inning. Kiley was batted out of the box in the fourth. Burns was also batted hard. Mudville played greatly in the field, but one error, a base on balls, being made. Flynn did fine work in left field, and Rabensky and Casey fielded well. Casey's batting was a feature. The score:

Barrett

They saw his face grow stern and cold, they saw his muscles strain,
And they knew that Casey wouldn't let that ball go by again.

rt C. Winthrop on the two han- dth anniversary of the company, June 838; ballots and bullets—the paper cur- y and metallic basis of a free ple! The former can only be

organist as they proceeded towards the altar, where she was joined by the groom, who had entered another door on the arm of the groomsman James Appleton. The ushers were Woodbury Kane, H. Curtis, Robert Perkins, William L. Green, Apple- ton Smith, Walter Bayliss, George Agassiz and C. S. Sprague. The bride wore a robe

of the many temptations to enter official life. He has left a brilliant reputation. H. C. Hutchins was chosen chairman, and C. A. Prince secretary. William G. Russell then offered a resolution that a committee of five be appointed by the chair to prepare a suitable expression of the sense of the bar upon the character of the deceased

tory—if it could be called a victory—had been won by the party who had brought politics into the fight. The respon- sibility rested with the Republican party. The contest which had been m would be pro

DUNLAP,
(CAPT. PITTSBURG).

The sneer is gone from Casey's lip, his teeth are clenched in hate;

He pounds with cruel violence his bat upon the plate.

CONDEMNED BY 60,000 MEN.

The Mills Bill and Its Advocates Denounced by Organized Labor.

PITTSBURG, June 2.—At the meeting of the Trades' Assembly of Western Pennsylvania, representing 60,000 organized workmen tonight, resolutions were unanimously

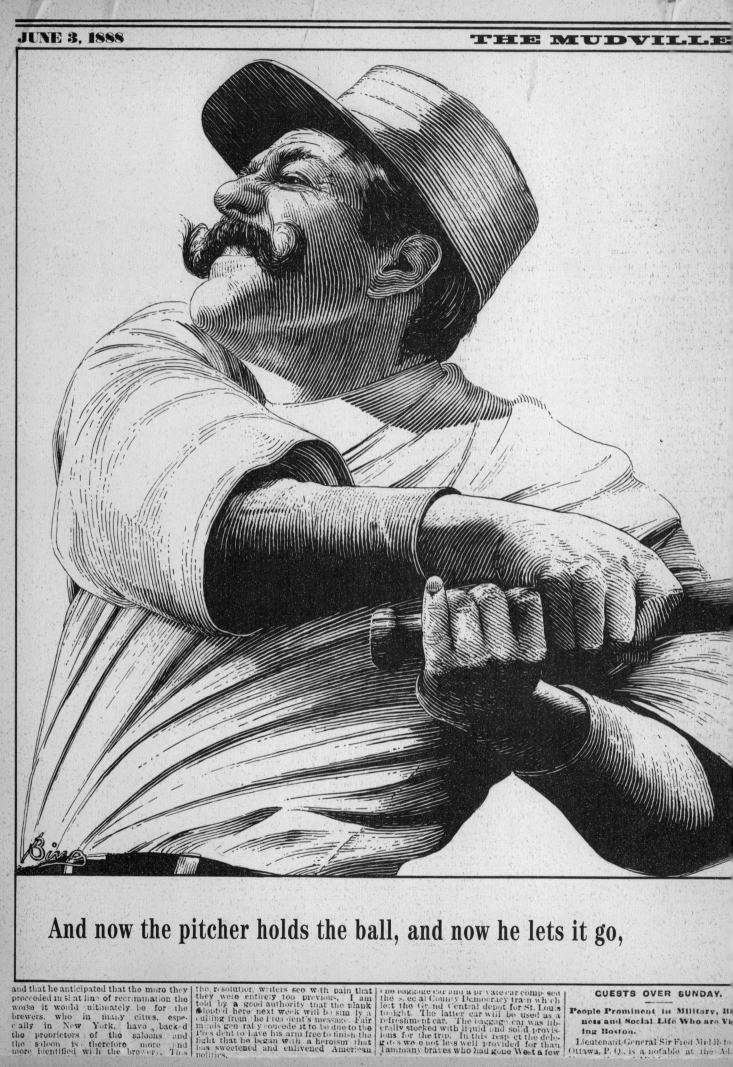

And now the pitcher holds the ball, and now he lets it go,

And now the air is shattered by the force of Casey's blow.

g the Republicans a good deal of le, if they had yet got down to seriously consider it. But I don't hear much in either party about the temperance matter this year. Now then a Democrat will say Republican friend that "your party will only two issues after a time, prohibition and protection." But the clear question

peculiar aspects to the vice president situation. For a year there have been two or three active and aggressive candidates in the field for this place, that is generally unsought; but there has been no national interest in these rather local characters and their aspirations. Nobody cares particularly for Gray, who has been the leading candidate. He is not a figure in the

Columbus, June 2.—A number of delegates to the Democratic national convention called at Senator Thurman's residence this afternoon, prior to leaving for St. Louis, but no meeting was held relative to taking action towards his support for vice president. Only about one-half the delegation was here. Judy Sherman will not go to St. Louis.

ance at the Country Club races yesterday, accompanied by Lady Middleton.

Prominent among the military men at Young's are General John B. Reed of Cotuit and Colonel Harry Hale of Bradford. Both gentlemen attended the reception in Music Hall last night in honor of our English and

Oh, somewhere in this favored land the sun is shining bright;
The band is playing somewhere, and somewhere hearts are light;

SURE TO BE THURMAN.

se of the Delegates All Pointing to Thurman's Nomination.

. Louis, June 2.—The newspaper men about the only visitors in St. Louis who day any eager interest in the Demo-

possible. An Indianian whispered that Thurman's name and a speech at Indianapolis would do more good in Hoosierdom than Gray's nomination. Red bananas are beginning to wave in front of headquarters, and Tammany will march behind this familiar symbol of the eminent snuff-taker of Columbus.

Just the same, it is a mighty cruel thing to

would add strength to the ticket, and would secure Indiana to the Democrats without a doubt. No formal action was taken, however, and the delegation will map out its course at a future meeting.

The name of Thurman of Ohio was mentioned, and while his past services to the party and to the country were highly and warmly commended, it was generally

Painters and plumbers now at w

—Today is the day to sample celebrated ice cream, there is noth

—Messrs. Hollis, Cobb & Co. ar with their speedy in a very stylish at her new quarters at No. W. street. The inner man and the fever are both catered to, a sto bringing rapid returns from ev

—The two old Commonwealth